LANDSLIDES AND AVALANCHES
in Action

Louise and Richard Spilsbury

rosen publishing's
rosen
central
New York

Published in 2009 by The Rosen Publishing Group Inc.
29 East 21st Street, New York, NY 10010

Copyright © 2009 Wayland/The Rosen Publishing Group, Inc.

First Edition

Editor: Susie Brooks
Managing Editor: Rasha Elsaeed
Designer: Tim Mayer
Picture Researcher: Shelley Noronha

Library of Congress Cataloging-in-Publication Data

Spilsbury, Richard.
  Landslides and avalanches in action / Richard and Louise Spilsbury. -- 1st ed.
    p. cm. -- (Natural disasters in action)
  Includes index.
  ISBN 978-1-4042-1868-0 (library binding)
  ISBN 978-1-4358-5138-2 (paperback)
  ISBN 978-1-4042-7879-0 (6-pack)
  1. Landslides. 2. Avalanches. I. Spilsbury, Louise. II. Title.
  QE599.A2.S747 2008
  551.3'07--dc22
                            2007043388

Photo credits: Cover, 4, Bckgd 2-3, 10-43 ©Geotechnical Control Office, Hong Kong Government; Bckgd 4-7, 44-45 ©Dan Dzurisin/USGS; 1, 20-21 ©Corbis Sygma; 5 ©Erik de Castro/Reuters/Corbis; 6 ©Christophe Boisvieux/Corbis; 7 ©Hbf/Lechner/epa/Corbis; 8 ©Galen Rowell/CORBIS; 10-11 ©Tom Casadevall/USGS; 12 ©Fernando Llano/AP/Pa Photos; 13 ©AFP/Getty Images; 14-15 ©AFP/Getty Images; 16-17 ©Reuters/Corbis; 18 ©Corbis Sygma; 19 ©Corbis Sygma; 22-23 ©AP/PA; 24 ©CORBIS SYGMA; 25 ©MIN.DE DEFENSE/AUT/CORBIS SYGMA; 26-27 ©Dieher Endlicher/ AP/PA Photos; 28-29 ©Reuters/Corbis; 30 ©Reuters/Corbis; 31 l & r ©Reuters/Corbis; 32-33 ©Kathy Hall; 34-35 ©Marcos Delgado/epa/Corbis; 36 ©Ulises Rodríguez/epa/Corbis; 37 ©Daniel Leclair/Reuters/Corbis; 38-39 ©AP/PA Photos; 40-41 ©Rex Features; 42 ©Reuters/Corbis; 43 ©AFP/ Getty Images; 44 ©Aurora/Getty Images; 45 ©Ashley Cooper/CORBIS

Manufactured in China

CONTENTS

What is a landslide?   4

What is an avalanche?   6

Triggering flow   8

CASE STUDY: NEVADO DEL HUILA, COLOMBIA, 1994   10

CASE STUDY: SARNO, ITALY, 1998   16

CASE STUDY: GALTUER, AUSTRIA, 1999   22

CASE STUDY: OROSI, COSTA RICA, 2002   28

CASE STUDY: PANABAJ, GUATEMALA, 2005   34

CASE STUDY: MOUNT KANGURU, NEPAL, 2005   40

Prediction, preparation, and prevention   44

Glossary   46

Further Information and Web Sites   47

Index   48

What is a landslide?

Imagine if the ground suddenly dropped from under your feet, or a sea of rubble came crashing into your home from a nearby hillside. That is what can happen during a landslide. Landslides occur when large amounts of surface cover break off and slip, roll, or fall down a slope. Slopes may be made of, or just topped with, materials such as rock, soil, mud, or ash from a volcanic eruption. Large landslides can sweep up trees, cars, and buildings in their path and bury entire villages at the bottom of a slope.

This landslide in Hong Kong killed 67 people when it demolished a 12-story apartment building. The disaster was triggered by heavy rainfall.

Types of landslides

Landslides are given different names depending on the type or size of material that has shifted. Large chunks of rock that break off and tumble down cliffs or steep slopes are called rockfalls. Lahars are mudflows that happen when ash from a volcanic eruption mixes with water, usually after heavy rain, to form a thick river of mud.

The impact of a landslide varies. Some landslides are small and have little effect on the slope below. Others are enormous, or start small but grow bigger when slipping material dislodges and carries with it even more debris. Large landslides can cause severe destruction, moving like express trains through settlements and other parts of downslope environments.

TUMBLING TOP SPEED

Landslides can travel at over 260 feet (80 meters) per second—much faster than a Japanese high-speed bullet train!

Weathering

Loose material forming landslides is often a result of weathering. This is the slow, gradual breakup of the surface rock. It is sometimes caused by the impact of tiny bits of sand or rock that are thrown against a surface by wind or moving water. It is also caused by the freezing and thawing (melting) of ice. Water expands (takes up more space) when it freezes. This can force open tiny cracks in rocks. The growth of plant roots can have a similar effect. Weathering can also happen when soft, crumbly rock is gradually dissolved by rainwater. Soil and mud form from pieces of weathered rock, bits of plant, or animal waste and water.

Landslide hotspots

Landslides happen anywhere in the world with steep slopes and weathering. Many occur in high mountain ranges, such as the Andes, Rockies, or Himalayas. Landslide hotspots (places where they are most likely to occur) include sheer cliffs, icy peaks, and particularly steep-sided river valleys called gorges. Other hotspots are in regions where volcanoes erupt, such as on land around the Pacific Ocean.

Many landslides occur along coasts, following intense weathering by ocean waves that wear down the rock at the base of cliffs. The rock higher up a cliff, and the soil on top of it, collapse without support. There is often a telltale pile of debris at the foot of sea cliffs. Similarly, land can collapse in areas with particularly soft rock, such as limestone. Occasionally, deep holes called sinkholes can suddenly appear in the land after underground rock weathers and the surface falls in.

This house in the Philippines crashed down into the sea after the cliffs it stood on fell down in a landslide caused by a typhoon.

What is an avalanche?

An avalanche is a mass of snow and ice that suddenly slips away from where it was resting and tumbles quickly down a mountainside. A small avalanche may be barely noticeable in the high mountains, but a larger avalanche crashes into or buries everything in its path. A large avalanche produces enough force to knock over and carry down anything from trees and buildings, to mighty boulders and vehicles. Avalanches and the heavy objects they carry with them can cause massive destruction.

SKIING DANGERS

Avalanches create most havoc where lots of people do winter sports. Nearly 80 percent of all avalanche deaths happen in France, the Unites States, Austria, and Switzerland, which are popular destinations with skiers and snowboarders.

Snow cover

Snow falls from clouds when temperatures are low enough to freeze the droplets of water in the atmosphere. Snow falls as little rounded granules or as intricate, star-shaped flakes, depending on the temperature of the air. Pieces of snow build up on top of each other, and those at the bottom change shape and settle into position depending on the amount of snow piled above them. The points of snowflakes generally mesh together and settle, forming strong, stable layers. However, granules roll over each other and settle in weak, unstable layers.

An avalanche of snow, such as this one in Nepal, can roar down a mountainside at 186 mph (300 kph)!

Avalanches can hurl cars down slopes and bury roads, animals, and entire towns under mounds of heavy snow.

Avalanches happen when unstable layers move. Any snow that has built up above the unstable layer becomes part of the avalanche. When temperatures are low, many separate stable layers of snow may build up on top of an unstable layer. Together, the snow cover can reach depths of many feet.

Types of avalanche

The most common types of avalanche are slab avalanches. These happen when thick snow cover shatters and breaks, much like a pane of glass, into jagged slabs that slide downhill. Dry slab avalanches move quickly because dry snow cover is light. Wet slab avalanches occur after bouts of rainfall or sunshine that loosen and weaken large snow slabs. Wet slab avalanches move more slowly, because the snow cover is wetter and heavier. However, the wet snow sticks to trees, soil, and boulders, and drags them along with it. The snow can also set hard when it stops moving.

Triggering flow

Road builders sometimes undercut slopes, making the rock and soil unstable and more likely to form landslides. Landslides can be triggered by vehicle movements, too, and also by the noise and vibrations of explosives used in mining or bombs.

Landslides and avalanches happen only when something triggers their flow. On slopes, any snow cover, soil, or rock will stay in place as long as friction is great enough. Friction is the sticking force between the underlying slope and the weight of material on top of it.

Losing friction

Friction varies with slope angle, roughness, and type of cover. For example, there is less friction on a smooth rock slope than on a rougher, plant-covered slope, and less beneath an unstable snow layer than a stable one. There are three main factors that reduce friction and trigger the flow of a landslide or avalanche—increased slope steepness, vibrations (shaking), and increased weight of slope cover.

Changing slopes

Slopes can change naturally. For example, they may become steeper when floods or waves wash away soil or rock, or following earthquakes. People change slopes, too. For example, when construction workers remove rock from slopes to build roads, they create unsupported overhangs of rock that might fall. Trees are often cleared from slopes to create space for ski runs, farmland, and new housing. Removing this cover reduces the friction and obstacles on slopes that would otherwise slow or block some landslides and avalanches.

Making vibrations

Earthquake movements and the force of erupting volcanoes may cause the ground to shake enough for surface cover to start moving. Other natural triggers of movement include fast gusts of wind. Avalanches are sometimes caused naturally by the movement of wild animals over snow, but most are caused by people. In an area with unstable snow cover, anything from the shout of a climber or skier, to the noise and juddering of a snowmobile engine may set off an avalanche.

Adding weight

Landslides are generally caused by heavy rain making the surface material wetter and heavier. This explains why most landslides happen during monsoon and hurricane seasons. Landslides are also triggered by volcanic eruptions that drop tons of loose rock or ash on slopes. Avalanches commonly strike when temperatures are warm after heavy snowfall. This causes thawing below unstable snow layers, which decreases friction with the snow or ground beneath.

SLIPPERY SLOPES

A third of landslide events in the U.S. happen on slopes that have been cleared of trees, usually for housing developments.

The yellow areas on this map show avalanche hotspots, and the red dots represent the locations of some of the worst landslides in recent history.

NEVADO DEL HUILA, COLOMBIA, 1994

Nevado del Huila is a mountain in Colombia with multiple peaks that were formed by ancient volcanoes. Running through the volcanic hills is the steep-sided Río Paez valley and along the bottom of the valley is a river. On June 6, 1994, an earthquake shook the ground beneath the southern edge of these mountains. The earthquake killed two people and damaged some buildings near the epicenter (the place where the earthquake started). But the real catastrophe happened in towns and villages along the river, where landslides triggered by the earthquake caused terrible damage and devastation.

QUAKE SCALE

The Nevado del Huila earthquake lasted for 40 seconds and rated 6.4 on the Richter scale. The Richter scale is an international system for measuring the size of earthquakes, in which 1 is the weakest and 10 is the strongest.

LANDSLIDE LOSSES

- Up to 2,000 people killed
- 20,000 people made homeless
- 6 bridges and more than 62 miles (100 km) of roads destroyed
- 2 villages completely buried

The first landslides

The earthquake struck at 3:47 p.m. Within minutes, the impact of the shaking ground had caused dozens of landslides, which swept swiftly down the steep valleys. Layers of unstable rock, ice, snow, and volcanic ash—which had gradually built up on the sides of the volcano from previous eruptions—slid down into the river below. This material had been made much wetter and heavier by intense rains in the recent rainy season, so it moved quickly and mixed with the water to form fast-moving streams of mud.

A lahar forms

As they flowed into the river, all the different streams of mud and debris soon combined into one huge lahar. The combined total volume of the Nevado del Huila lahar was estimated at 60 cubic miles (250 cubic km). That would be enough to fill about 250,000 Empire State buildings! This heavy, fast-moving lahar quickly progressed and grew as it picked up more and more debris, including trees and boulders, which it swept along as it hurtled toward towns lower down the river.

The lahar that flowed down the Río Paez valley and beyond looked like a river of heavy wet concrete. In some places, the flows reached 98 feet (30 meters) high. The mud traveled at 50–65 feet (15–20 meters) per second—much too fast for people to outrun. Close to the valley, the direct impact and weight of the lahar ripped huge boulders, trees, and houses from the ground and carried them along with it. Farther downstream, the lahar simply covered everything in its path in a deep, sticky layer of dense black muck. Just ten minutes after the earthquake had struck, villages were buried in mud.

The devastating lahar that swept through Nevado del Huila in 1994 left huge, brown scars on the landscape.

NEVADO DEL HUILA, COLOMBIA, 1994

River of rock

People who survived this disaster described the mudflow that roared down the valley toward them as a black wave of death. The residents of the valley were mostly members of Native American communities, who made their living by farming the valley slopes. There were casualties and fatalities, as well as other damage, in the villages of Irlanda, Toez, Talaga, and Paez Belalcazar. Many of the survivors were left huddling together on freezing mountain slopes, some of them trapped by shifting mud that was simply too dangerous to cross. Homes, schools, businesses, and community buildings, such as churches, hospitals, and health centers, were destroyed. Overall, the population affected by the widely felt earthquake and the more restricted mudflows numbered an estimated 50,000.

The village of Paez Belalcazar was almost completely buried in mud.

MOSTLY MISSING

Of the almost 2,000 people that were killed by the Nevado del Huila mudslide, only 271 bodies were found. Around 1,700 were defined as missing, presumed dead, and buried under the mud.

Evacuees look down sadly at the mud-choked land that used to be their community. Many people were made homeless by the disaster and needed new places to live.

Emergency rescue

Emergency service workers and members of the Red Cross came to the area immediately to take part in a rescue operation. Their work was made much more difficult by the mountainous terrain. Also, the lahar had cut off land access to the area by blocking or damaging roads and bridges. The only way to rescue people wounded or stranded by the mudflow was by using army and police helicopters.

Many injured people were successfully evacuated by helicopter to hospitals, and others were sheltered in a large number of camps. However, rescue workers often put their own lives in danger, and five Red Cross workers died when shifting mud trapped them as they tried to get to victims.

EYEWITNESS

On June 7, 1994, the archbishop of Paez Belalcazar, Jorge Garcia, flew over the landslide area. He observed that the village of Toez had been almost completely buried in mud, saying "only the roof of the school can be seen."

The aftermath

After the initial rescue efforts, it was time to help survivors stay alive. Airplanes and helicopters were used to bring in food, kitchen utensils, medicine, and shelters such as tents or plastic sheets. Blankets and bedding were also flown in to protect people from the mountain chill, along with bottled water, because water pipes and supplies had been wrecked. The president of Colombia appealed to the people of his country to donate money, food, and clothing to help the victims of the disaster who had been made homeless. Donations of chainsaws were also requested, for people to use to cut down wood for fuel.

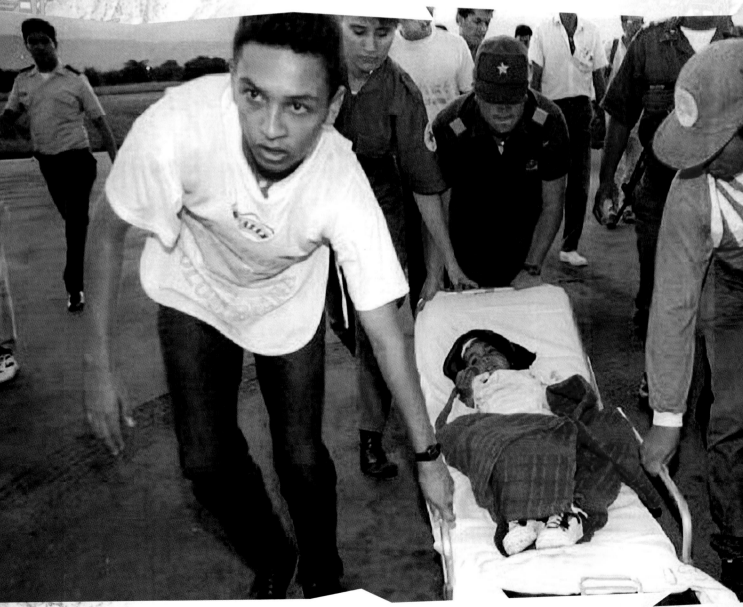

Could more people have survived?

After the horror of the disaster became clear, some people said that fewer would have died if they had understood the signs. An approaching lahar makes a huge rumbling noise and often makes the ground vibrate, too. After the earthquake, many people in the Río Paez valley mistook these as signs of an aftershock, or smaller secondary earthquake, and stayed where they were. If they had known the real cause of the noise and juddering, they may have had time to get to high ground before the lahar reached them. More lives could be saved worldwide if people who live in valleys below volcanic mountains moved to high ground for a few hours immediately after an earthquake, just in case a destructive mudflow were to head in their direction.

Since the Nevado del Huila mudslides, the United Nations has been working with Colombia to help protect people against future disasters—for example, by providing training on managing emergency situations, educating people about disaster awareness, and mapping areas that might be at risk from landslides.

The first priority after a disaster is to get injured victims to the hospital, but it is also vital to provide other survivors with water, food, and shelter so that their lives are not put at risk, too.

UN REPORTS

These are notes from United Nations reports summarizing the state of emergency at different points in time:

JUNE 8
Report number 2: Press reports 150 people may be missing.

JUNE 8
Report number 3: 2,500 affected, of which 1,000 are inhabitants of two villages swept away by avalanches; casualties increasing.

JUNE 9
Report number 4: National mobilization campaign for food and relief items organized through the media.

JUNE 10
Report number 5: Landslides have killed some survivors. About 13,400 people could be affected.

JUNE 12
Report number 6: So far, 267 tons of relief supplies lifted in flights to affected areas.

JUNE 14
Report number 7: About 14,000 affected people receiving relief assistance.

JUNE 21
Report number 8: Emergency conditions prevail in disaster area, where rains continue.

JULY 8
Report number 10: Thousands of people continue to stay in makeshift camps. 2,800 people involved in relief work.

SARNO, ITALY, 1998

Sarno is a town near Naples, in southwest Italy, built on the lower slopes of Mount Sarno. The underlying rock of this mountain was coated in thick volcanic ash after ancient eruptions of a nearby volcano, Mount Vesuvius. The volcanic soil is fairly loose and unstable on the slopes, so the area has a history of landslides. At the beginning of May 1998, Sarno experienced two days of torrential rain that triggered four devastating mudslides. The disaster left 118 people dead and hundreds of homes damaged or destroyed.

A Sarno resident is rescued by helicopter from the roof of his collapsed house. In the background are the slopes of Mount Sarno, where the mudslides began.

LANDSLIDE LOSSES

- 118 people killed (at least 97 of these from Sarno)
- More than 1,500 people made homeless
- 300 homes damaged or destroyed
- Estimated cost of damage: $500 million

Background to a disaster

The soil that is formed from volcanic ash is very fertile. Forests grow naturally on Mount Sarno's slopes, but over the centuries, people have cleared the trees to create farmland to grow grapes, olives, and other crops. This has caused the slopes to become more unstable, since tree roots naturally hold the soil together. Small mudslides and flooding in the nineteenth century led the rulers of Sarno to protect the town. They ordered basins (large dips in the ground) and drainage channels to be dug on the cleared slopes. These protected the town by helping to catch, slow, or redirect moving mud and water.

In the second half of the twentieth century, the slopes of Mount Sarno were less well cared for. People started many forest fires to clear more land of trees, in order to encourage the growth of grass and other low plants for their livestock to graze on. Heavy grazing in some areas completely killed off plants, leaving bare slopes.

Later, people concreted over the channels and basins on the slopes to construct roads and houses. In Sarno itself, they built more and more houses on the river banks in the center. In the past, people had avoided this low-lying area because they knew river flooding could damage any houses there. After small landslides in November 1997 and January 1998, many people said there was a major disaster waiting to happen in Sarno.

The slides begin

As the rain poured down on Sarno in the days leading up to the mudslides, water soaked through the soil on the slopes, making it heavy. There was so much water that some formed rivers between the mountain rock and the overlying soil. At first, streams of dirty water flowed off the mountain, but eventually the soil washed completely off the underlying rock. This formed a 23-foot (7-meter) high wave of mud that washed down and swept through the town.

Impact

It is estimated that as much as 3 billion tons of mud slid off the mountain slope toward Sarno. The thick mud wave traveled at speeds of around 19 mph (30 kph). It knocked down and carried along everything in its path, from boulders 6.5 feet (2 meters) across to trees 50 feet (15 meters) high. The first houses to be picked up or knocked down were on the slopes above Sarno.

The path of destruction continued down to the river, the lowest point in the town. The enormous volume of mud and debris forced the water out of the river, flooding houses along the riverbank. The river water also made the mud more liquid. This thinner mud flowed even faster and spread through the houses in the town, because the river was blocked and the mud had nowhere else to go.

The mudslides swept through streets, washing away cars and destroying or damaging many buildings.

Mud invasion

In Sarno, the liquid mud forced open doors and caved in windows, filling ground floor rooms up to the ceiling. Some people fled to the upper floors of their homes and managed to escape, but others were buried under the debris of the buildings when the force of the mud knocked down the lower walls. On the streets, hundreds of cars were washed away like toys, and power lines were knocked down, causing severe electrical hazards.

When the mudslide slowed, the wet mud started to set hard. The mud particles pushed and clung together, forcing water out of the gaps between them. People and their possessions became stuck in the mud.

Some parts of Sarno were badly damaged, but others remained intact. This statue in a resident's garden survived the impact.

A tale of two towns

Several towns in the area around Mount Sarno were hit and partially buried by mudslides on May 5, but Sarno suffered the most casualties. In nearby Quindici, many houses were ruined by the mud but only 11 people died. This is less than a tenth of the number who died in Sarno. In Quindici, the authorities had realized the risk of landslides following heavy rain and evacuated the citizens at noon. In Sarno, however, the mayor told the people that everything was under control and ordered no evacuation. Environmental groups, such as the World Wide Fund for Nature (WWF), believed that this was not so much a natural disaster as one caused by many years of bad land management and a lack of awareness of the real danger in which people were being placed.

EYEWITNESS

〝 It sounded like an earthquake. But it was not the earth moving. It was the air. 〞

Febo Carillo, a Sarno resident who heard the sound of the air pushed out of the way by the speeding mud

Relief effort

The first rescuers to arrive on the scene were volunteers from nearby areas. People from farther away struggled to reach Sarno, because many main roads were blocked by mud and debris. Over the next few days, the number of rescuers and helpers rose to around 4,000. They included firefighters, doctors, and nurses, and military personnel including U.S. Marines stationed in nearby Naples.

The rescue workers used spades to dig out survivors and dead bodies from the mud. They located them and then carefully removed building rubble to release trapped survivors. This work was very dangerous, because rescuers were at risk of being trapped in the mud, injured by debris, or falling into deep gaps in the rubble. Medical workers gave first aid to the wounded and took the seriously injured to local hospitals.

EYEWITNESS

❝ Reconstruction has been very slow, sometimes nothing at all—completely stopped. ❞

Giuseppe Ruggero, local charity worker

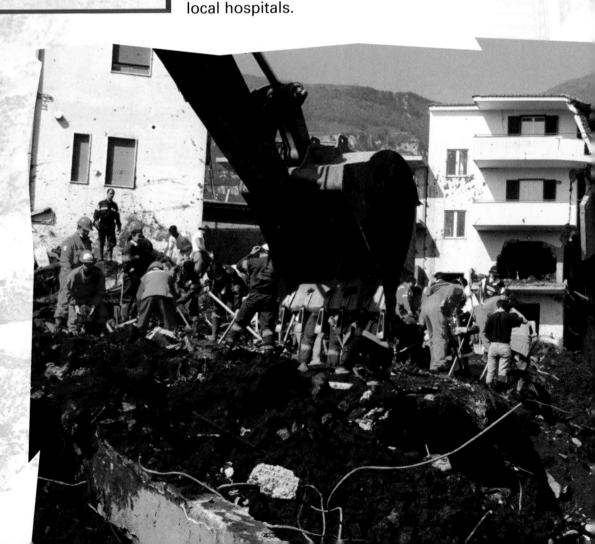

IGNORING THE MUD

Not all life in Sarno was transformed by the disaster. Relief volunteers were angry to discover that in some places that had escaped the mud, people who could have been helping were actually relaxing in cafés drinking coffee and chatting the day after the disaster!

Clearing up the mud and debris after a mudslide of this scale is a huge, expensive and time-consuming operation.

Coordination

The U.S. Marines cleared mud from the streets with army bulldozers to allow more rescue vehicles and workers to reach the survivors. The town authorities set up a command post in the city hall to organize the relief effort. Here, volunteers answered telephone calls and e-mails from people worried about relatives. The main Sarno school and market areas were transformed into giant shelters for the homeless. Volunteers cooked food, gave out blankets, and spent time talking with the shocked and injured survivors.

Recovery

The homeless survivors could not return to Sarno for many months after the mudslides, because their homes were mud-filled or unsafe to enter. Some stayed in local apartments, but many had to remain in the temporary shelters. Parts of Sarno remained in ruins for years after the disaster, but by 2006, life was mostly back to normal. Crops were growing in farmland once cloaked in thick mud, and most buildings had been cleaned up, repaired, or rebuilt. However, because the rebuilding of Sarno took such a long time, some people left the town to start new lives elsewhere. For example, Episcopio was the part of town worst hit by the mudslides. Of the 5,000 people who lived there before the disaster, 1,500 moved away for good.

The Sarno disaster woke the authorities to the dangers of landslides in southern Italy. Two years later, in December 2000, officials forced more than 500 people to evacuate their homes and closed major roads as a precaution after a period of heavy rain that might have increased the threat of mudslides.

GALTUER, AUSTRIA, 1999

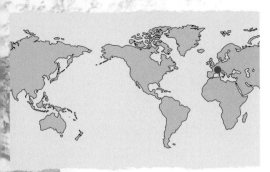

The village of Galtuer (pronounced gawl-ture), near Innsbruck, lies in the Paznaun valley in Austria, close to the Swiss border. The valley is famous for its snowy slopes and is extremely popular with skiers. During the ski season, the relatively small local population of around 700 people swells with an extra 3,000 visitors. In February 1999, there were even more tourists here than usual because there had been a large amount of snowfall, the most for 50 years. No one predicted that this snowfall would lead to a disaster that took more than 30 lives.

Dangerous conditions

By February 23, the snow was so unusually heavy that Galtuer had been cut off from neighboring villages for days. Throughout western Austria, up to 20,000 people had been trapped in mountain resorts by snowfalls up to 13 feet (4 meters) deep. In addition, the weather conditions at the time were hazardous. Freeze-thaws, in which snow melted and froze again, meant that weak layers of snow were forming on the slopes. Strong winds with speeds of up to 56 mph (90 kph) had also blown vast amounts of snow into towering snowdrifts, which meant that large piles of unstable snow were gathering high in the mountains in some areas.

EYEWITNESS

❝ We were drinking hot, mulled wine, when suddenly it started. The lights went out. It was dark. There was only dust and snow. We got out of there as fast as we could. ❞

Franz Wenko, hotel operator in Galtuer

The residents of Galtuer found their village covered by a thick blanket of snow in the winter of 1999.

Sudden impact

Suddenly, the weight of all the unstable snow became too much for the slopes' friction to support. At 4:00 p.m. on February 23, a huge avalanche fell down the mountainside above Galtuer. As it raced downhill, a wall of snow and ice traveled at 180 mph (290 kph); it took only 50 seconds to reach the bottom of the valley. When it hit the village, the avalanche was up to 330 feet (100 meters) high, 1,640 feet (500 meters) wide, and so powerful it sliced the tops off houses and buried homes. Nearly 60 people were trapped.

AVALANCHE HISTORY

The location of Galtuer beneath steep, snowy mountains has meant a history of local avalanches. The worst on record happened in 1689 when 250 villagers were killed. In the 1999 avalanche, 31 people died. It was one of dozens of avalanches to strike central Europe as the region endured its heaviest snowfall in 50 years.

GALTUER, AUSTRIA, 1999

Aftermath

Austria is a more economically developed country (MEDC), so it has the money and resources to deal rapidly with disasters such as this avalanche. Even so, it took 16 hours for outside relief workers to arrive in Galtuer. Snow was still falling heavily, making it impossible for helicopters to fly in, and earlier avalanches had blocked the main roads. During the first few hours after the disaster, local firefighters, police, and volunteers had to deal with the situation unaided.

The avalanche left vast quantities of snow on the valley floor, making it very hard for rescue vehicles to get through to Galtuer.

Rescuers focused their efforts on searching near buildings, because people trapped in homes had a better chance of survival than those buried in the open streets.

AVALANCHE LOSSES

- 31 deaths
- 7 buildings destroyed
- 28 buildings damaged
- 1,700 people evacuated

First rescue efforts

The snow from the avalanche set hard like concrete, and rescuers dug desperately through it using any implements they could lay their hands on. They poked long metal probes down into the snow to detect survivors. Luckily, there was also one local dog, called Heiko, who was trained to sniff out people buried under masses of snow. There was no time to waste, because people were at risk of hypothermia and of running out of oxygen in the confined spaces in which they were trapped. In the first day, rescuers managed to dig out about 20 people, many of whom were critically injured.

Flight plans

On the second morning, helicopters began to fly between nearby Landeck and Galtuer. Extra helicopters were sent from the United States and Germany to help with the relief effort. At Galtuer, the helicopter teams dropped off food, such as fresh fruit and vegetables, for people who stayed in the village. They also collected injured victims and survivors wrapped in blankets and transported them to hospitals. At Landeck, there were buses waiting to take tearful tourists to an army camp where they could speak to a counselor, to help them recover from the shock and horror of their experience. From there, vacationers left for home by train.

A safe place?

By February 28 (day five), roads to and from the valley had been cleared. Also, the threat of more avalanches was practically over, as warmer temperatures steadily began to thaw the snow on the mountainsides. By this time, 31 people had been confirmed dead and their angry families were asking why the avalanche had reached the village when Galtuer was supposed to be safe.

There were snow fences on many slopes in the Paznaun valley, built to hold snow in place and stop it slipping. But these were not deemed to be necessary in Galtuer. Since there had been no evidence of avalanches reaching the village for centuries, it was designated a safe, or green, zone (see box). Other avalanches had followed the same route as this almost every year, but they had never reached as far as the village because Galtuer is over 656 feet (200 meters) away from the bottom of the mountain. Tragically, in 1999, the avalanche picked up twice its initial volume of snow as it traveled down the mountainside, making it bigger than any other avalanche in the area for more than 200 years.

HAZARD ZONES

In most populated regions of the Alps, areas are divided into avalanche hazard zones.

- **RED ZONE: No building allowed because the area is at high risk of avalanches.**

- **YELLOW ZONE: Moderate risk; buildings are allowed here, but must be made of reinforced concrete to resist avalanche strike.**

- **GREEN ZONE: Avalanche safe; buildings are allowed to be built here; no reinforcement is required.**

AVALANCHE SAFE

Avalanche-proof houses have reinforced concrete walls and no windows on the sides that face the mountain slopes.

Galtuer survives today, protected by sturdy avalanche barriers and with new, stronger buildings in place. But will all this be enough to prevent future disasters?

Improved protection

In Galtuer since the disaster, $20 million have been spent on avalanche protection structures and the avalanche hazard zones have been extended. Steel snow fences have been erected on mountain tops to prevent avalanches starting there. New houses and other constructions have to be built to avalanche-proof standards. On the valley floor, there is now a 985-foot (300-meter) long avalanche wall to protect Galtuer. Today, the village remains an important snowsports center, but the event has made people even more aware of the ever-present dangers.

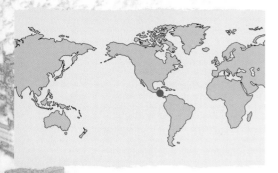

OROSI, COSTA RICA, 2002

Orosi is a small town in central Costa Rica, Central America. It lies at the base of one of the most beautiful valleys in the country, flanked with steep hills. During heavy rains, the area is vulnerable to landslides as loose soil is washed down the slopes. At dawn on Saturday, August 31, 2002, hundreds of thousands of cubic feet of mud and debris slipped down the hills into Orosi. The mudslides, powered by tropical downpours, drenched the valley and town.

FARMING CHANGES

Farmers used to grow coffee under forest trees, where the shade prevented the beans from being damaged. Today, forest trees are being cut down on coffee plantations, because newer types of coffee do not need the shade and are easier to harvest in the open.

LANDSLIDE LOSSES

- 7 people killed
- 23 homes completely destroyed
- More than 400 people made homeless

The Orosi valley in Costa Rica is fringed with coffee plantations.

Tropical seasons

Costa Rica is a tropical country on the narrow isthmus (strip of land) connecting North and South America. It has just two seasons. The dry season, between late December and April, has very little rain. The rest of the year is very wet, with regular heavy storms. The wet season is often called the "green" season, because it is the time during which plants grow most rapidly. The green season is also the time when landslides on the Orosi hills threaten the settlements below.

Sodden soil

The mountains above Orosi are coated with very fertile soil, formed from ancient volcanic dust and rock. This soil, the wet and warm climate, and the steep slopes together provide ideal conditions for growing coffee. In recent years, many poorer farmers have cleared small patches of land to grow coffee and other crops. In addition, larger plantations that have been in the area for a long time have changed their land use slightly. They have moved from growing coffee bushes among trees and other plants, to growing just coffee bushes. Removing the natural vegetation and its roots from the hillsides has made the soil less stable. An added problem is that the farmers dump uprooted trees in gorges when they have cleared the ground. This has blocked several of the usual drainage routes for rainwater runoff from the hills. Therefore, the soil has become more waterlogged and heavier than usual.

By August 2002, about halfway through the green season, the soil on the hills above Orosi had soaked up a lot of water. Three consecutive days of endless, heavy rain at the end of the month proved too much for the slopes to stand. The land began to slide, choking the valley and the village with a torrent of sticky mud.

Rescue and repair

It did not take long for news of the Orosi disaster to spread. As soon as the alarm was raised by townspeople, the Costa Rican Red Cross sent in 120 workers to carry out a search-and-rescue operation. Their work was hampered by continuing heavy rain until September 4. This washed the mud from the landslide and spread it throughout the town.

The force of the moving soil damaged water and sewage pipes. When sewage mixes with flood water, this causes an obvious health hazard. The Costa Rican Red Cross distributed containers full of clean water. They also gave out filters to strain dirt from the flood water, and tablets to kill bacteria and other organisms in the water, so that it was clean enough to drink. These had to be used until the mud was cleared up and pipes were repaired.

The giant mudslides that poured down a gorge into Orosi buried homes under deep, shifting mud.

STATE OF EMERGENCY

The Costa Rican government officially declared the situation in Orosi after the mudslides an emergency. They gave 100 million colons (about $275,000) to help the town.
Each of 43 affected families received 300,000 colons ($820) to buy household items and furniture, and 50,000 colons ($137) to buy food. The government also paid to rebuild housing for the families.

Landslide spreads disease

In tropical countries, diseases caused by bacteria and viruses often spread quickly. This is because both the disease-causing organisms and animals, such as insects, that spread the disease thrive in the humid conditions. One of the most dangerous infectious diseases in Costa Rica is dengue. The symptoms of dengue include fever, headache, joint pains, rashes, and vomiting. It can often kill very young, old, or sickly people. The disease is caused by a virus that is transmitted when mosquitoes bite people.

After the landslide, the ground in and around Orosi was very uneven with debris and piles of soil, and there were lots of extra dips where rainwater collected. This created thousands of puddles where mosquitoes could lay eggs and develop. In the week after the mudslides, doctors in Orosi reported 400 new cases of dengue. During the wetter weather in central Costa Rica, mosquitoes infected with dengue spread inland.

The bite of a dengue mosquito can make a person very sick. Disease spread throughout Orosi as these insects thrived and bred in the warm, wet conditions.

Additional effects

In Costa Rica, the landslides had many effects apart from destroying homes, causing disease, and injuring or killing people. They ruined many coffee plantations and small-holdings, so farmers could not earn a living selling coffee. Damage to the environment and to amenities, such as hotels, restaurants, and roads, also put off tourists who usually visited the area to see wildlife and ancient temples nearby.

Continued rain kept the mud sticky and very difficult to clear from the streets.

OROSI, COSTA RICA, 2002

Early warning

Costa Rica decided to establish an early warning system for landslides following the Orosi disaster. Four centers were given radio equipment that people could use to hear weather reports and to call for help after a landslide. A landslide warning siren was installed on a large telecommunications tower built on the hill overlooking the town.

CARING FOR THE LAND

The Ecoamigos Program, founded by Professor Carlos Mata, was taught in Orosi schools in the months after the landslides. Youngsters played games and carried out fun activities to learn the importance of caring for local trees, rivers, and wildlife. For example, they found out that removing forests to make way for coffee plantations reduced the variety of bird and animal life.

In Orosi today, schoolchildren learn about mudslides and how to look after the surrounding land in the hope of preventing future landslides.

❝ When the... landslide hit the hillsides of Orosi, the town was able to stick together and recover from the natural disaster. ❞

Amy Chan, Sustainable Development in Costa Rica, 2004

Being prepared

The Costa Rican Red Cross set up a community training program so that locals would be better prepared. Red Cross workers gave courses in first aid for volunteers in the community. They trained volunteers to deal with distressed survivors after disasters. The Costa Rican government worked with scientists and teachers to inform the community about how to prevent landslides in the future. They taught farming families that cutting down trees can make landslides more likely and that planting quick-growing trees and bushes can make slopes safer.

May 23, 2003

Nine months after the first disaster, there was another landslide in the region. This time the Orosi community responded much more quickly. During heavy rains, locals used their radios to access up-to-the-minute weather information. The government warned that landslides could happen if rains persisted. So, the mayor of Orosi sounded the sirens. This was the signal for people in the town to evacuate. Again soil, trees, giant rocks, and other debris crashed down the hillside. Some homes were damaged and destroyed, but this time no one was killed. After the event, local people worked as an efficient team alongside Red Cross professionals to care for the homeless. Everyone remained on alert for further landslides while the rain persisted.

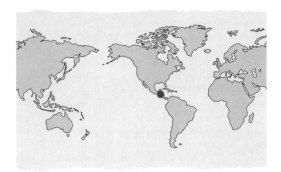

PANABAJ, GUATEMALA, 2005

At around 4:00 a.m. on October 5, 2005, a loud, deep, rumbling sound echoed around the volcanic mountains above the village of Panabaj in Guatemala, Central America. The small village, home to 3,000 Mayan Indians, had already suffered days of torrential rainfall brought by Hurricane Stan as it passed through Guatemala, El Salvador, and the surrounding regions. Suddenly the soaked, loose ground gave way and a landslide .6 mi. (1 km) in width crashed down the slopes of the volcano above the village.

Panabaj is about 100 miles (160 km) west of Guatemala City, the country's capital. The deadly landslide left the village covered in mud up to 40 feet (12 m) deep in places.

LANDSLIDE LOSSES

- 1,000 people declared missing and presumed dead in Panabaj (fewer than 80 bodies recovered)
- About 5,000 people made homeless

Lost village

The landslide of water, mud, and sand swept across the village, burying people and buildings in as much as 20–40 feet (6–12 meters) of liquid earth. It cut a deep canyon through the mountainside, and carried tree trunks and boulders the size of small cars into the village. Some people who woke in the middle of the night and heard the rumblings from the volcano's slopes managed to escape, but others were buried alive when the wall of mud crushed their homes, trapped them in their houses, or swallowed them up as they fled. About a third of residents were killed.

History of a hurricane

Hurricanes happen regularly in Central America's tropical climate. Stan was the eighteenth tropical storm in the 2005 Atlantic hurricane season. Although it was only a Category 1 hurricane, which means it was low strength, it still blew violently and brought with it an enormous quantity of rain. Hurricane Stan began on October 1 over the Caribbean Sea and died, or ran out of energy, on October 5 after hitting Panabaj. Overall, in all of Central America, flooding and mudslides triggered by Hurricane Stan left 500,000 people homeless and up to 2,000 dead.

WHAT IS A HURRICANE?

Hurricanes are strong winds that start over warm oceans when warm, humid air rises fast and cold air quickly blows in to take its place. The rising air cools, creating clouds. The air rises faster and faster, eventually forming fast-spinning storm clouds. Hurricanes continue as long as they remain over warm water, which gives them the energy to keep spinning.

PANABAJ, GUATEMALA, 2005

Rescue and relief

The people living in Panabaj were mostly poor farmers, growing coffee and other crops on the volcanic soils of the region. Many of them lived in makeshift houses built out of sheet metal and sticks, and these fragile homes were easily destroyed. After the landslide, little could be seen other than the tops of lampposts and trees poking through the mud that had crushed the village.

In the first two days after the disaster, the only people helping survivors were locals. Hundreds of villagers stumbled over the drying mud with shovels, picks, axes, broom handles, and branches to dig for victims. It was difficult work. As the mud dried, it set hard but the ground was still so unstable that rescuers risked falling into holes themselves while they searched. The mudslide had been so immense that it was difficult to know where to look.

Boulders, branches, and other debris carried by the landslide lay scattered over the mud-smothered village.

Shelters for survivors

Rescue workers from outside the area, who were unable to get through any sooner because the roads had been blocked by mud, only reached Panabaj on Friday—two days after the disaster. Many families who had managed to flee the landslide were taken to shelters, such as churches in a nearby town, but conditions were very cramped and uncomfortable. Rescue efforts were also hampered by the lack of medical facilities.

The only hospital in the area, which had just reopened after being closed for 15 years as a result of killings during a civil war, was hit by disaster again when it was buried in mud by the landslide. Bad feeling among Mayan Indians toward the Guatemalan army as a result of their part in the civil war meant that soldiers were not encouraged to help with the relief work.

Many of the rescuers who dug for survivors were local villagers with only hand tools to help them.

International aid

Help from abroad arrived four days after the mudslide, because the weather had prevented flights into the area until then. The United States and Mexico sent helicopters, and other aid included water treatment systems (to make dirty or contaminated water safe to drink) and medical supplies. By the following Tuesday, improved weather allowed boats to cross Lake Atitlán to ferry supplies to survivors. Many foreign tourists were evacuated on foot and by helicopter.

PANABAJ, GUATEMALA, 2005

A mass grave

Most of the people that rescuers managed to dig out from the mud were already dead, and on Tuesday, October 11, exhausted rescue workers gave up their efforts. The bodies were rotting so quickly in the mud that they could no longer be identified if they were found, and there were serious concerns that digging out the bodies would only spread disease. At this point, the area that had once been a village was closed off and declared a mass grave.

Families of the victims paid their respects at the site of the village after it was declared a mass grave.

Reviewing the disaster

Mudslides are a regular hazard on the steep hillsides of Guatemala. The country is in a tropical region and has regular rainy seasons when the slopes become soaked and saturated topsoil slides away. Knowing this, why do people still live in high-risk areas? The problem is that Guatemala is a less economically developed country (LEDC) with many poor people—almost 40 percent of the population lives on less than $2 a day. Many people make a living from farming the fertile land on the slopes and have no choice but to live in danger zones, because land in safe places is bought up by the small minority of the Guatemalan population that is wealthy.

Loss of tourism

As well as farming, another source of income for many Guatemalans living around Lake Atitlán is tourism. The beautiful, clear blue waters of the lake draw many visitors to the area. Mayan Indians make money, for example, by making and selling colorful masks, fabrics, and other crafts, or by acting as guides to tourists. But after the mudslides, months passed before Lake Atitlán received any new visitors. On the anniversary of the disaster, in 2006, people in the region were still suffering a loss of income from the fall-off of tourism and the destruction of farming lands.

DISASTER DAYS

OCTOBER 3, 2005
Hurricane Stan swirls toward Mexico. Hurricane warning is issued across the Gulf Coast.

OCTOBER 4
Stan slams into Mexico's Gulf Coast and drives storms across Central America, causing flooding and landslides.

OCTOBER 5
Landslide buries Panabaj.

OCTOBER 6
In Panabaj, 15 bodies are pulled from the mud but continuing rains hinder search efforts.

OCTOBER 8
Officials estimate 508 people are dead, with 337 missing.

OCTOBER 11
Authorities in Guatemala abandon efforts to recover bodies and focus on helping the survivors, who have lost everything.

OCTOBER 2006
About 1,000 families in Panabaj are still living in shelters. Many are still out of work. Across Guatemala, 11,000 people are still waiting for the government to build them new homes.

JANUARY 2007
Families of victims persuade the authorities to dig up buried bodies. More than 100 have been found.

MOUNT KANGURU, NEPAL, 2005

Millions of avalanches happen around the world each year, but most go unnoticed because they occur high in remote mountains where no one lives. Mount Kanguru, in the Himalayas of Nepal, is the eleventh largest mountain on Earth and one that is inaccessible and difficult to climb. Few people will ever have witnessed an avalanche on its slopes. But on October 20, 2005, a group of experienced climbers was caught up in a fatal fall of snow.

ADVENTUROUS CLIMBING

Many of the highest peaks in the world are in the Himalayan mountain range, which runs from Pakistan in the west, across the top of Nepal to eastern Tibet (China). The Himalayas attract hundreds of climbing trips every year. Climbers use the short period between the end of the monsoon rains in September and the onset of winter to attempt any ascent of Himalayan mountains in Nepal.

Tackling Mount Kanguru

Mount Kanguru stands 22,900 feet (6,981 meters) high, near the Annapurna region of the Himalayas. In October 2005, the leading French mountaineer, Daniel Stolzenberg, seven other climbers, and a team of Nepali Sherpa guides and porters set off on an expedition to climb it. The team members were experienced and very well prepared, taking with them plenty of survival equipment. They chose to set off in the fall because this was usually a safe season, before the greater buildup of snow in winter. All went well initially—the weather was cloudy with mild winds—but conditions suddenly deteriorated on October 20, when a heavy snowstorm hit the mountain. The team's tent camp was in a steep-sided valley under a rocky ridge where snow was building up. One Sherpa porter suggested moving it, but the others were not convinced there was a real danger.

Avalanche!

Late that afternoon, at around 4:00 p.m., expedition members had finished their dinner and were settling into their tents. Suddenly, a massive avalanche swept down the slope and smashed straight into the camp. All seven French members of the team and 11 of the porters were swept up and buried by a mass of deep snow.

The impressive snow-capped peak of Mount Kanguru rises up above the clouds.

DISASTER DAYS

OCTOBER 20, 2005
Avalanche sweeps away 18 people on Mount Kanguru.

OCTOBER 23
Four surviving Nepalese porters are rescued.

OCTOBER 25
Rescue team with 20 French and Nepalese members flies to the avalanche site. Body of one French climber is recovered from the snow. Other climbers are officially declared dead since any hope of finding them alive is lost.

NOVEMBER 1
Body of a second French climber is found.

NOVEMBER 5
Search for remaining bodies is postponed because weather conditions are too harsh.

JUNE 2006
Search efforts resume seven months after the tragedy when the snow has melted.

JUNE 12
Bodies of the remaining climbers are found.

Aftermath

Out of the team of 22 on the Kanguru expedition, only four Sherpa porters survived the disaster. Luckily, they had been standing outside or in a kitchen tent a little lower down the mountain when the avalanche struck, so they had been able to get out of its way just in time. Their tents were swept away, with all their mountain equipment inside. They walked barefoot to alert rescue teams before being admitted to hospital with severe frostbite on their toes. The Himalayan Rescue Association and the French government put together rescue teams to search for survivors. However, no one held out much hope of finding anyone alive because there was simply so much snow.

EYEWITNESS

ʺ All Dawa Lama [one of the surviving Sherpas] remembers is a loud boom and immediately after that a terrific whoosh. When he regained consciousness, he was lying 98 ft. (30 m) away from camp. ʺ

Padam Ghale, rescuer, *Nepali Times*, Issue 306

Rescuers searched in vain for survivors in the deep snow. Heavy snowfall meant that visibility was poor and there was a real danger that the rescuers might be hit by an avalanche themselves.

Rescue tactics

The French rescue team used sniffer dogs on the mountain to try to locate the lost climbers. Rescuers dug bravely through the ice and debris dumped at the bottom of the valley by the avalanche. Someone carried a satellite phone, so they could call for a helicopter should they find any survivors, but helicopters were no help in searching for people, because the snowfall was too heavy to see the ground below. The search continued for days. By October 25, the goal was reduced to recovering bodies since all hope was lost of finding anyone alive. The rescue team believed that the bodies of the missing climbers had been carried into a mountain gorge by the snow and that it would be almost impossible to locate them.

Photos and tributes to the people who lost their lives on Kanguru in 2005 are displayed at a memorial in their honor.

This proved to be the case. Eventually, the search was abandoned and the bodies were not recovered that winter. However, the snow began to melt in late spring, and by summer, some of the bodies were found and could be returned to their families to receive proper funerals and farewells.

Looking to the future

The families of the French climbers who died found a way of consoling themselves in their grief by setting up the French Solidarity Kanguru Association (FSKA). The foundation pays to educate the 23 children of the dead Nepali Sherpas in Kathmandu boarding schools, and provides money and skills training for their mothers to help them build a future for themselves and their families.

Prediction, preparation, and prevention

Landslides and avalanches can be enormous events, affecting wide areas and involving many communities. They cannot easily be stopped, but experts are researching better ways of predicting and preparing for them, to limit the damage and deaths that they cause.

Predicting events

Geologists use aerial photographs and GPS to study changes in slopes where landslides could happen. GPS uses sensing equipment on satellites to record changes in the position of receivers put on slopes. These intricate systems can detect movements of mere inches in a year, and can identify the exact area of ground that is moving. Geologists also record changes in slope steepness, and the wetness and weight of soil and other material on slopes that might start a landslide.

Geologists cut sections of snow to study how the type and moisture content of different snow can result in an avalanche.

There are many avalanche institutes worldwide that assess slopes for avalanche risk. They collect weather data and information about the type of snowfall in the area. One way of assessing snow type is to dig pits in snow to see how the layers have settled. Snow that is unstable and has not settled tightly has air spaces in it, and often sounds hollow when it is tapped.

Avalanche breakers such as these break up the snow in an avalanche before it reaches villages in the valley floor below.

SIGNS OF SLIPPAGE

When land starts to slide, it affects the ground, buildings, and other features downslope. Here are some clues that a landslide may be on its way:

- **new, widening cracks or bulges in pavements**

- **sticking windows and doors, as a result of twisting door and window frames**

- **tilting telegraph poles or trees**

- **damp patches of ground or water bubbling to the surface after water pipes have broken.**

Preparing for the worst

In some places, landslides are a constant threat, and people prepare their slopes. They build tough metal fences to catch rockfalls, and plant trees to help stabilize the soil. When building in landslide areas, people may use flexible plastic pipes for water or sewage, because these can move without cracking. People may prepare emergency packs of equipment, such as a flashlight, food, and a radio to help them survive in the event of a landslide. Families learn evacuation routes so that they can escape to safety.

The best way of preventing avalanches is to remove unstable snow on high slopes, usually by triggering small avalanches on purpose. People use rifles or gas-powered cannons called avalaunchers to "shoot the slopes." Communities in avalanche zones often build strong avalanche breakers to stop snow slide. People who regularly go out onto the slopes, such as rangers and ski guides, may carry transceivers that produce radio signals so that rescuers can trace them even under snow.

Glossary

aftershock Ground shaking caused by underground rocks repositioning after an earthquake.

atmosphere The layer of air surrounding Earth.

bacteria Small, single-celled organisms, some of which can spread disease.

civil war A war fought between groups of people from the same country.

debris Scattered material, such as tree branches or building rubble, that has been dislodged or broken and left behind after a landslide, avalanche, or other disaster.

donations Money, food, and other useful things given by people to others.

drainage channels Ditches that allow water to drain off land.

earthquake Shaking of the ground caused by underground movement of rocks.

epicenter The point on the Earth's surface immediately above an earthquake.

evacuate To move away from a dangerous place to somewhere safe.

fertile Describes land capable of growing many, healthy plants.

freeze-thaw A type of weathering caused by expansion of ice in cracks in rock.

friction A force resisting motion between two substances that are in contact, for example, a layer of rock and overlying soil.

geologist A person who studies the Earth and rock formations.

GPS Global positioning system, allowing accurate location of points on Earth using sensors on satellites.

humid When the air is moist.

hurricane A tropical storm with winds faster than 75 mph (120 kph).

hypothermia A dangerous loss of body warmth that can result in death.

lahar A landslide of volcanic ash mixed with water, forming mud.

LEDC A less economically developed country (one where average income for people is very low and industry is sparse).

Mayan Indian A member of a Native American tribe.

MEDC A more economically developed country (one where average income for people is high and industry is plentiful).

monsoon A seasonal wind that blows across Asia bringing heavy rains.

plantation A large farm with many workers growing one crop for sale.

reinforced concrete Concrete made stronger by containing steel rods.

satellite A scientific object that revolves in space, usually carrying equipment that can transmit signals to and from Earth.

saturated Full of water.

Sherpa A member of the Himalayan people of Nepal and Tibet, who are known for their skill as mountaineers.

tropical Relating to the region of Earth on either side of the Equator that is warm and usually humid.

tropical storm A powerful storm developing over warm tropical seawater.

typhoon A term used for a hurricane that occurs in regions around the Pacific and Indian oceans (also called a cyclone).

vegetation The range of plants in a place.

virus A tiny organism that multiplies within the body and causes disease.

volcano An opening in the Earth's surface through which molten rock, steam, and ash may rise and accumulate, often forming mountains.

Further Information

Books

Avalanche and Landslide Alert!
Vanessa Walker
Crabtree, 2004

*Awesome Forces of Nature:
Crushing Avalanches*
Louise and Richard Spilsbury
Heinemann, 2003

*Awesome Forces of Nature:
Thundering Landslides*
Louise and Richard Spilsbury
Heinemann, 2004

Disasters Up Close: Mudflows and Landslides
Michael Woods and Mary B Woods
Lerner Publications, 2006

Web Sites

Due to the changing nature of Internet links, Rosen Publishing has developed an online list of Web sites related to the subject of this book. This site is regularly updated. Please use this link to access this list:
http://www.rosenlinks.com/nda/laia

Index

Numbers in **bold** refer to illustrations.

avalanche
  breakers 45, **45**
  casualties 23, 25, 26, 41, 43
  damage 6, **7**, 23
  debris 43
  hazard zones 26–7
  protection structures 26–7,
    27
  survivors 25, 42
avalanches 6–7, **6**, 8, 9, **9**,
  22–7, **24**, **25**, 40–3, 44, 45
  in Austria 22–7, **23**, **24**, **25**,
    27
  in Nepal **6**, 40–3, **40**, **42**
  slab 7

building construction 27, 45

climbers and climbing 40, 41,
  43, **43**
coffee production 29, **29**, 36

diseases 31, **31**

earthquakes 8, 9, 10–12, 15
Ecoamigos Program 32
environment, peoples' effect
  upon 8, **8**, 9, 17, 28–9
evacuation responses 13, 15,
  19, 21, 33, 37, 45
evacuees **13**

flooding 35
freeze-thaws 22
French Solidarity Kanguru
  Association (FSKA) 43
friction 8, 9, 23

geologists 44, **44**
GPS (global positioning
  system) 44

hurricanes 9, 34, 35, 39

lahars 4, **10**, 11, 12, **12**, 15
landslide
  casualties 12, **13**, **14**, 16, **16**,
    19, 20, 29, 35, 38, 39
  damage **4–5**, 12, **12**, 18,
    18–20, 30, 36, **36**
  debris 11, 18, 20, 28, 31, 33,
    36
  hotspots 5
  in Colombia 10–15, **10**, **12**,
    13, **14**
  in Costa Rica 28–33, **28**, **30**,
    31
  in Guatemala 34–9, **34**, **36**,
    37, **38**
  in Italy 16–21, **16**, **18**–20
  landslides 4–5, **4–5**, 8, 9, **9**,
    10–21, 28–39, **30**, **31**, **37**, 44,
    45
  survivors 12, 14, **14**, 20–1

monsoon rains 9, 40
mudslides *see* landslides

Native American people 12,
  37, **37**, 39

poverty and natural disasters
  39
prediction 44–5
preparation **32**, 33, 44–5
prevention 33, 44–5
protection 17, 44–5

rebuilding and recovery **20**,
  21
rescue operations 13, 14, **14**,
  16, 20–1, 24–5, **25**, 30, 36–8,
  37, 41, 42–3, **42**
Richter scale 10
rockfalls 4, 45

sanitation 30
shelters 21, 37, 39
Sherpas 41, 42, 43
sinkholes 5
snow and snowfall 6–7, 22,
  23, 25, 41, **42**, 43, 44, **44**, 45
state of emergency 15, 30
Stolzenberg, Daniel 41

typhoons **5**

volcanic eruptions 4, 9
volcanoes 5, 10, 11, 16, 34

warning systems 32–3, 45
weathering 5
winter sports 6, 22